Mother Teresa

Helping the Poor

MOTHER TERESA

William Jay Jacobs

The Millbrook Press
Brookfield, Connecticut
A Gateway Biography

Cover photo courtesy of Agence France Presse/Corbis-Bettman

Photos courtesy of Susan Greenwood/Gamma-Liaison: frontis; Earl Kowall/Gamma-Liaison: pp. 8, 21 (bottom); Yugoslav National Tourist Office: pp. 11, 14 (bottom; the Loretto Sisters: pp. 14 (top), 18, 21 (top); Francois Lochon/Gamma-Liaison: p. 23; Francolon/Gamma-Liaison: pp. 25, 26 (top), 29; Wide World: pp. 26 (bottom), 33 (bottom), 37, 38 (both), 42 (bottom); UPI/Bettmann: p. 33 (top); Pablo Bartholomew/Gamma-Liaison: pp. 35, 42 (top); Laurent Maous/Gamma-Liaison: p. 41; Agence France Presse/Corbis-Bettman: p. 44.

Library of Congress Cataloging-in-Publication Data
Jacobs, William Jay
Mother Teresa: helping the poor / by William Jay Jacobs
p.   cm.—
Bibliography p.
Summary: Mother Teresa was a nun working in Calcutta, India. She dedicated her life to doing what she could to help those who suffered from loneliness and poverty. She received the Nobel Peace Prize in 1979.
ISBN 1-56294-020-1 (lib. bdg.) 1-878841-57-2 (pbk.)
1. Teresa, Mother, 1910–1997. 2. Missionaries. 3. India. 4. Charity. I. Title.
B (92) 1991

Published by The Millbrook Press, Inc.
2 Old New Milford Road
Brookfield, Connecticut 06804

Leave your country, your people, and your father's household and go to the land I will show you. I will bless you; I will make your name great, and you will be a blessing. I will bless those who bless you.

Genesis 12:1–3

Mother Teresa

The poor of Calcutta, India, are often forced to live on the streets. Mother Teresa devoted her life to helping such people.

Sunrise in Calcutta, India. For some 200,000 people who have spent the night in fitful sleep on the city's streets it is the dawn of a new day. Like all other days, they will spend it searching, clawing, for a few scraps of food to eat.

Summer and winter—in wind, rain, heat, and cold—old and young alike sprawl alongside buildings, clothed only in tattered cotton rags. Sometimes they huddle together on the center island of a traffic circle. There, scarcely taking note of their misery, an endless stream of cars and buses, motorbikes and rickshas, whirls round their tiny cooking fires. They live in the traffic circles. They die in them.

Death is everywhere. Old people, often deserted by their families, are too weak even to beg for a few rupees—a little money—to buy food. The sick are left to die, with no one to care for them.

Beggars plead to every passerby for *baksheesh*—help for the poor. A visitor who takes pity finds himself surrounded at once by crowds of onlookers pressing their claims, too, for "One rupee, please, sahib"—something—anything to stay alive.

Cows, meanwhile, considered holy by the Hindu faithful, wander the streets untouched. Their ribs exposed from hunger, they poise delicately, like the poor around them, on the very brink of death.

It was just such a scene that greeted the young nun, now known to the world as Mother Teresa, when she first arrived in Calcutta in 1929 to begin missionary work among the poor of India.

She had been born Agnes Gonxha Bojaxhiu on August 27, 1910. The Macedonian town of Skopje, her birthplace, is now part of Yugoslavia but then was ruled by the Turks. A small group of Albanian Catholics lived there, including Agnes's father Nikola (Kole) Bojaxhiu and his wife, Drana.

Kole and Drana were deeply religious. They gave money to the Catholic Church. They tried to help poor people get food and shelter. Agnes, whose adult life was to be devoted to those causes, always remembered her father's teaching that she "never take a morsel of food that you are not prepared to share with others."

A street in Skopje, which is now in Yugoslavia. Much of the town was destroyed by an earthquake in 1963. But this section looks much as it did when Mother Teresa was a young girl.

In 1919, Nikola Bojaxhiu suddenly died. Before long the family's savings were gone. Drana found herself alone, faced with the need to support Agnes, then nine, and two older children: Lazar, a boy of eleven, and Aga, a girl of fourteen.

Drana became a seamstress, making dresses and embroidery for the wealthy women of Skopje. These women only recently had been her social equals. Faced with hardship, Drana showed great courage. Instead of being crushed by the loss of her worldly goods, she continued to share what little her family had with people who had even less. She invited the poor into her house and made them welcome. She visited the elderly, the sick, the lonely.

Drana made little public show of her acts of charity. As she told her children, "When you do good, do it without display, as if you were tossing a pebble into the sea."

It would be a lesson that Agnes, as Mother Teresa of Calcutta, would never forget. Drana, more than anyone else, impressed young Agnes with the idea that charity meant, quite simply, caring for others.

When Agnes later decided to become a missionary nun, her greatest regret was in having to leave home. "We were," she recalled, "a family full of joy and love, and we children were happy and contented."

Young Agnes Bojaxhiu learned much from her family. She also learned from the teachings of the Catholic Church. She and her sister, Aga, both sang in the church choir. They had such fine voices that they became known as "the two nightingales."

One priest in her parish, Father Jambrekovich, went far toward shaping Agnes's plans for her future career. He taught her in exciting detail about the work of church missionaries who helped the sick and the poor of Calcutta, India.

Agnes was twelve years old at the time. She began to consider seriously a lifetime of service to the church, working overseas as a missionary nun.

At the age of eighteen, Agnes Bojaxhiu announced her decision to become a nun. She applied to the Order of Loreto, whose missionary nuns worked in eastern India.

Agnes Bojaxhiu in 1928,
about the time that she
decided to become a nun.

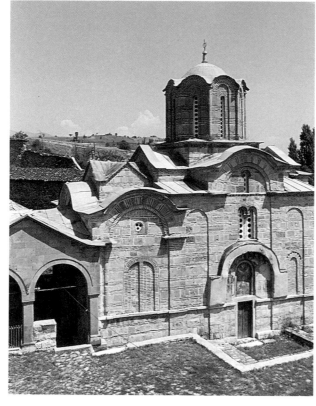

Religion was
an important
part of Mother
Teresa's child-
hood. This is
the monastery
of St. Mark in
Skopje, built
in the 1400s.

For Agnes, the decision had not been easy. She knew that she would have to give up her happy family life and go to a distant country. She would have to give up the idea of marriage, children, a family of her own. She was a gifted musician and a promising student with a special talent for writing. All of these would have to be sacrificed for the sake of service to others.

Agnes first had prayed for guidance. She had gone on retreats to a nearby shrine. She had sought the advice of priests and of her mother, Drana. It was only after all those steps that she had made her decision. With her acceptance by the Order of Loreto, all that remained was her farewells to family and friends in Skopje.

On learning of Agnes's decision, her brother Lazar was shocked. Lazar, who had just become an officer in the army of King Zog of Albania, wrote to her. Had she lost her senses, he demanded, giving up her freedom to go live in a poor country halfway around the world?

"Lazar," she replied strongly, "you think you are important because you are an official serving a king of two million subjects. But I am an official, too, and I serve the King of the whole world! Which of us do you think is in the better place?"

Lazar thought the matter over and, changing his mind, gave Agnes his blessing.

Drana, Agnes's mother, asked only that she be certain of her decision and that, once sure, "she strive only for God." Later, when Agnes was known to the world as Mother Teresa, she recalled her determination never to change her mind about becoming a nun. She knew her mother would ask, "Well, my daughter, did you live only for God?"

On September 25, 1928, she said good-bye to Skopje. Her music teacher recalled her departure, as the train for Zagreb began to leave the platform:

> The distant sunlight illuminated her briefly, and she seemed to us like the moon slowly vanishing in the light of day; growing smaller and smaller, still waving, still vanishing. And then we saw her no more.

At Zagreb, Agnes was joined by another girl, Betika Kajnc, who also had been accepted by the

Order of Loreto. Together they left for the Loreto Abbey in Dublin, Ireland.

Their reason for staying at the Abbey was to study English, the language they would teach schoolchildren in India. But they learned other things, too. They learned to wear the dress, or "habit," of the Loreto nuns. They learned to walk softly in the hallways of the Abbey.

Most important of all, they learned about silence. There was to be silence at the dining table while one of the sisters read aloud from the Bible or another book. And then, from bedtime to morning, came the "Great Silence." Not a word was to be spoken until the girls preparing to be nuns would awake and come together to hear Mass and take Communion.

It was at the Loreto Abbey in Ireland that Agnes Gonxha Bojaxhiu took on a new name, Mary Teresa of the Child Jesus. Betika, her friend, took the name Mary Magdalene. Having put their old names and their former lives behind them, the two young women were now ready for new lives as Catholic sisters.

In Ireland, Agnes took a new name: Mary Teresa of the Child Jesus. This picture shows her in 1930.

In January, 1929, after a long journey on shipboard, the two finally arrived in India. Almost at once they plunged into their studies. They improved their knowledge of English. They also learned Hindi and Bengali, the major languages of the area around Calcutta.

Soon afterward, Teresa's change of name became formal. Then, two years later, she took her first vows as a Sister of Loreto. She pledged herself to a life of poverty, purity, and obedience. As Sister Teresa, she began to teach and to help the nurses at a small medical station in northern India.

Next, she was assigned to teach at the Loreto convent school in a section of Calcutta. From her window in the convent she could look out on the ugliness of a slum, one of Calcutta's very worst neighborhoods. Yet inside the high walls of her school, alongside beautiful gardens and well-trimmed lawns, she taught history and geography to the children of the rich. She lived her life separate and apart from the poverty and filth everywhere around her.

In May, 1937, Sister Teresa took her final vows.

Once more she was accompanied by her friend, Betika, now known as Sister Mary Magdalene. Soon afterward the Head (principal) of the school retired, and Teresa took her place as Head, becoming for the first time "Mother Teresa."

She should have been happy. Yet, as she looked around her, she could not avoid seeing Calcutta's poor. She began to pray that, somehow, she could do more to help those who suffered so much. From Skopje, her mother, Drana, encouraged her, reminding her why she had gone to India in the first place—"to help the poorest of the poor."

Nine more years passed, nine years spent in the calm, peaceful religious life of the Loreto convent. Then, on September 10, 1946, while traveling by train for her annual retreat, something happened. Mother Teresa heard the voice of God.

As she later described the message, "I was to leave the convent and help the poor while living among them. It was an order. To fail would have been to break the faith."

A nun is supposedly called to that vocation by God. Mother Teresa ever afterward spoke of this new experience as "the call within a call."

Above: The Loreto convent school in Calcutta, where Mother Teresa taught and eventually became head, or principal.
Below: The Loreto convent was in the heart of Calcutta, but Mother Teresa had little contact with the poverty around her.

Because she had promised to spend her life serving the Loreto Order, Mother Teresa had to ask permission of her superiors to leave. What she hoped to do was start her own order of sisters—sisters who would live among the poor and share their lives. At first the authorities refused to let her do this. They did not think her ideas would work. Some of them did not think she could lead an order of sisters. One priest remembered that when she first became a nun "she could not even light the candles."

Mother Teresa prayed. She asked the help of priests with influence in Calcutta and in Rome. Finally, her request was granted. To her it seemed almost a miracle.

On August 16, 1948, she prepared to leave the convent. Laying aside the formal robe and stiff collar of the Loreto Order, she put on common sandals and a simple cotton sari with a blue border, the clothes of the poor women of India. Then, with the farewell songs of her students, sung in Bengali, still ringing in her ears, Mother Teresa closed the convent door behind her and stepped outside into the streets of the slum, alone.

A plain cotton sari, like those worn by the poor women of India, became Mother Teresa's dress. This picture shows her in 1986.

For three months she studied medicine with the Medical Missionary Sisters at Patna. She learned how to give injections; how to treat patients suffering from starvation; how to set broken bones; how to deliver a baby.

Then, just before Christmas, 1948, Mother Teresa returned to Calcutta. She had no place to stay and carried with her only five rupees—less than one U.S. dollar.

The Little Sisters of the Poor, an order whose mission was to care for the elderly poor, agreed to let her live with them. At first she helped the sisters in their work and prayed for guidance about her own mission in life. Then, one day, she simply began walking the streets of the slum.

After an hour, with five children by her side, she sat down in an open space beneath a tree. She smoothed a parched patch of earth and began writing the Bengali alphabet in the dirt with a stick. Curious, other children joined her. Soon there were thirty or forty.

Every day she taught the children in her outdoor school. She taught them the alphabet and how

From the beginning, children were especially important to Mother Teresa. Here she comforts an abandoned child.

*Above: Mother Teresa
sought out the sick and
dying on the streets.
Right: A dying man,
found on the street,
is helped to Mother
Teresa's shelter for
the dying in Calcutta.
The shelter was
founded to give poor
people a place to
die with dignity.*

to do simple arithmetic. She taught them how to use soap and water to clean themselves, rewarding good students with a tablet of soap. At midday she gave them containers of milk.

In the evening Mother Teresa would seek out people on the street—the sick, the elderly, the dying—and try to help them. Weary, her bones aching from overwork, she knew it was a time of testing for herself. She prayed for God's help:

> You, Lord, only You, all for You. Make use of me. You made me leave my convent where I was at least of some use. Now guide me, as You wish.

The work before her seemed endless. Crowds of people followed after her in the streets. They clutched at her sari, begging for food. Many tried to kiss her feet, hoping for help.

Surrounded by the clatter, the din of Calcutta's streets, she longed for the silence of the Loreto convent—its peace, its cleanliness. Instead, she found violence—stabbings and brutal robberies. There were children playing in human waste, piled in the street. There was vomit. There were cries of pain, of people without hope.

Through it all, Mother Teresa tried to remind herself that she was not helping a crowd of people, but one person at a time. And that one person was Jesus. When she soothed a starving baby, that baby was Jesus. When she put drops of water on the parched lips of an old man, she was nursing the Lord.

As she put it, "It is Christ you tend in the poor. . . . It is his wounds you bathe, his sores you clean, his limbs you bandage."

Through prayer, she spoke to God. "The comfort of Loreto," she said, "came to tempt. But of my own free choice, my God, and out of love for You, I desire to remain. Give me courage."

Mother Teresa worked on. She refused to return to the peaceful life of Loreto. And soon she found others at her side, helping. First there was Subhasini Das, one of her former students at the Loreto convent. From a wealthy family, Subhasini agreed to give up her many beautiful saris. She would own only two coarse cotton ones with a blue border, just like Mother Teresa's.

Others soon joined Mother Teresa in her work. She is seen here with two members of her order, the Missionaries of Charity.

She promised to live like the poor, without the comforts of her home and family. She would have enough food—but just enough and no more. Like Mother Teresa, too, Subhasini pinned a simple cross on the left shoulder of her sari. Then she chose a new name for herself—"Agnes"—because it was Mother Teresa's name before she had become a nun.

Other sisters joined Mother Teresa: Sister Gertrude, Sister Bernard, Sister Margaret Mary. An Indian Catholic, Michael Gomes, gave the upper floor of his mansion as a place for the sisters to live. They furnished it with packing boxes for chairs and an old crate for a desk.

In 1950, Mother Teresa applied to Rome, asking official recognition for her new order of nuns. Several months later a letter of approval came, establishing the Order of the Missionaries of Charity.

By then there were twelve sisters. Their daily life followed strict rules. They rose at 4:40 A.M. and immediately went to chapel for prayer. For breakfast they ate the simple Indian flat bread, *chapati.* From 8 A.M. to 12:30 they served the poor. Following lunch came meditation and prayer and then service to the poor again until 7:30 P.M. Supper was followed by evening prayers at 9:00 and bed at 9:45.

For many years Mother Teresa worked to ease the pain of sick people who were dying alone in the streets of Calcutta. She saw that hospitals would not accept patients too poor to pay. So they would simply return to the filthy streets to die. In 1952, Mother Teresa gained permission from city officials to use the back rooms of a former temple as a place to shelter the dying. She and the other sisters would carry people there, so that at least they could die with some dignity.

As Mother Teresa put it, "A beautiful death is, for people who have lived like animals, to die like angels—loved and wanted." Regardless of religion, the dying were always given medical treatment. They were washed and cared for. And they were given the last rites of their religion, whatever that faith might be.

By 1953 the Missionaries of Charity had moved into larger quarters. Their new home was a three-story building at 54A Lower Circular Road, an address that would become famous as the order's

Mother House. New sisters joined the community. As word of their kindly deeds spread, gifts of money and goods began to arrive from the outside.

Despite her order's growing success, Mother Teresa still refused to be called by her rightful name, "Reverend Mother." She insisted on working alongside the younger sisters, never asking them to do what she herself would not do. She scrubbed the floors on her hands and knees. She washed out the toilets. She laundered the bedding in pails of water.

In 1955, Mother Teresa opened *Shishu Bhavan*, a home to care for children. Some were newborn babies, left to die in the streets or on garbage heaps because their parents could not care for them. Of those, many did not survive. But before they died, they were soothed and loved by Mother Teresa and her nuns.

Many babies who had been brought to *Shishu Bhavan* starving and helpless miraculously recovered. After a week or two of tender care they smiled—some of them for the first time in their lives. Mother Teresa brought them up as members of her family.

Above: Mother Teresa takes a quiet moment at the prayer hall of her order's Mother House before beginning her daily rounds. Below: At Shishu Bhavan in Calcutta, orphaned and abandoned children are cared for by the Missionaries of Charity.

She also took in orphans from the street. Some grew to adulthood with her. For the boys she provided education. For the girls *Shishu Bhavan* became the setting for their marriages, with Mother Teresa providing cakes and sweets and even arranging a dowry—a gift to the groom—according to Indian custom.

Nor did Mother Teresa forget the most outcast souls of all, the lepers. These were people who suffered from leprosy, a terrible disease that attacks the nerves and the skin. Without treatment, leprosy can cause weakness or paralysis, even the loss of toes, fingers, and other parts of the body.

Since biblical times lepers had been shunned, avoided by the rest of society, because people feared catching the dreaded disease. In 1957, Mother Teresa opened *Shanti Nagar* (leper town), a secluded place where lepers—even those who had lost fingers or hands—could learn a trade and support themselves.

When a new medical treatment for leprosy was discovered, Mother Teresa carried on a campaign to spread the news to victims. She urged them to come in at first sign of the disease, so they could be

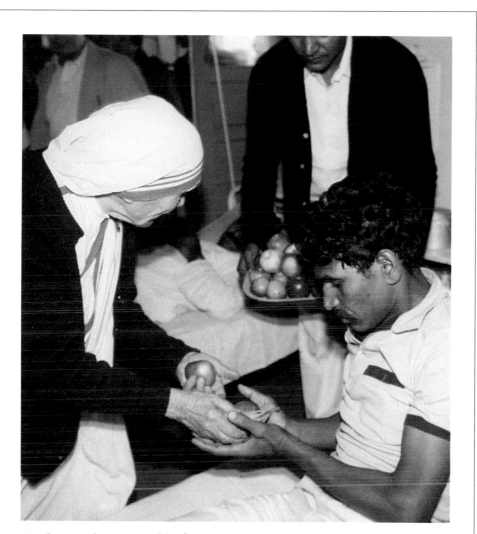

As her order grew, Mother Teresa continued to work alongside the sisters in caring for the sick and the poor. Here she visits a victim of a chemical plant accident in Bhopal, India, in 1984.

cured. For those who came too late, the nuns at *Shanti Nagar* provided care and tenderness and, in some cases, a pleasant place to die.

The fame of Mother Teresa and her community of sisters now began to spread. Nuns and priests from other orders came to join her. From all over India volunteers found their way to Calcutta to help in her work. Many were Hindus and followers of other non-Catholic religions. In 1963, Mother Teresa even organized a missionary order for men. They would work among the poor in places where women could not go.

In time, Mother Teresa expanded the work of the Missionaries of Charity to include other countries. She opened new houses to help the poor in countries such as Venezuela, Italy, Tanzania, Australia—even in Great Britain and the United States. By 1990 there were some 430 homes in 95 countries around the world.

Mother Teresa traveled from continent to continent. At first, paying for the airfare proved troublesome, since she had no money of her own. Once

Mother Teresa at the opening of a new chapter of her order in Phoenix, Arizona, in 1989. There are chapters in 95 countries.

Above: Greeting children in Belfast, Northern Ireland, in 1971.

Right: Escorting Indian orphans to new homes in Rome, Italy, in 1979.

she even asked if she could pay her way by working as a stewardess! Hearing of the amazing request, India's prime minister, Indira Gandhi, arranged for a free pass for her on all flights of Air India, worldwide. After that, she enjoyed sitting in silence on her many trips, hurtling through the air at hundreds of miles an hour, saying her rosary.

Once, when the Pope visited Calcutta, people presented him with an elegant white Lincoln Continental limousine. At the end of his trip he turned it over to Mother Teresa. She promptly raffled it off and gave the money to her home for lepers.

From around the world honors and prizes poured in upon her. Always, in receiving the awards, she spoke of herself as "unworthy." She used the occasions to express her belief in God and to raise money for the work of her order.

Once, while in London to receive an award, she encountered an old man, walking the streets on a bitter cold night. "Take me, take me anywhere," he said to her. "I am longing to sleep between two sheets." To Mother Teresa it was a lesson. The world must learn, she said, that the poor are not only in Calcutta. Maybe there are not so many in

England. Yet "even if it is one, he is Jesus, he is the one that is hungry for love, for care." Mother Teresa knew that she alone could not remove the causes of poverty. Yet she dedicated herself to doing what she could.

In 1979, Mother Teresa was given the Nobel Peace Prize. She accepted the award in Oslo, Norway, speaking with simplicity to the elegantly dressed crowd gathered to see her. "People must love one another," she said, "so nobody feels unwanted, especially the children."

As she grew older, her body stooped ever so slightly. Her face, burned brown from years in the hot sun of India, now was creased with lines. In Albania, her mother, Drana, and her sister, Aga, both had died. Yet Mother Teresa did not seem old or weak. "To meet her," said Indira Gandhi, "is to feel utterly humble, to sense the power of tenderness and the strength of love."

*T*hose *ideas were* at the heart of Mother Teresa's life. And they will live on through the people who worked with her, built with her, believed in her.

Mother Teresa displays her Nobel Peace Prize at the award ceremony in Oslo, Norway, in 1979. A $190,000 check that accompanied the award was sent to India to help the poor.

Mother Teresa consciously, and gladly, set out to live a life of struggle. To triumph required great sacrifice on her part but the reward for her—far greater than her worldwide fame—was the reward of satisfaction. Perhaps the great Bengali poet of Calcutta, Rabindranath Tagore, best expressed the pleasure of those saintly few who sometimes live among us:

> I slept and dreamt
> That life was joy
> I awoke and saw
> that life was duty
> I acted and behold
> Duty was joy.

Although a Catholic nun living in the largely non-Christian land of India, she made no attempt to convert those around her to Christianity. Religion to her was a way to bring together life on Earth and life in Heaven. She saw prayer as a tool for helping people to face their problems on this planet in preparation for what she hoped would come afterward to all. And she taught both Christians and non-Christians to actively spread love to others. Above all, she wanted people to enjoy their lives by dealing directly with God, as she declared that Jesus had done.

All human beings eventually must die. Mother Teresa knew that she too would someday pass from existence on this planet. And, according to her, she looked forward to death. "We only surrender our body in death—our heart and our soul live forever."

"When we die," she said, "we are going to be with God, and with all those we have known who have gone before us: Our family and our friends will be there waiting for us."

She concluded by saying that: "We must live each day as if it were our last so that when God calls us we are ready, and prepared, to die with a clean heart."

On September 5, 1997, Mother Teresa died. She was buried inside the headquarters of the religious order she had founded many years earlier. Hers had been a life devoted to helping others. By working so hard, she called the world's attention to those in need. For this she deserves to be remembered with reverence for many years to come.

*Mother Teresa received a state funeral in India,
an honor usually reserved for the highest-ranking
government officials.*

Important Dates

August 27, 1910	Agnes Gonxha Bojaxhiu is born in Skopje, Macedonia
September, 1929	Begins missionary work in India
May, 1931	Begins teaching at the Loreto convent school in Calcutta
May, 1937	Takes final vows of service to the Church
December, 1948	Opens her school for children in the slums of Calcutta
October, 1950	Officially becomes head of the Missionary of Charity
1952	Establishes a house for the dying in Calcutta
1955	Establishes *Shishu Bhavan*, a home for children in Calcutta
February, 1965	Begins to expand work of Missionaries of Charity to countries outside India
December, 1979	Awarded Nobel Peace Prize
September 5, 1997	Mother Teresa dies

Further Reading

If you want to learn more about Mother Teresa, there are several fine books you might like to read. Some of them are:

Mother Teresa, by Joan Graff Clucas (Chelsea House, 1988).
Mother Teresa, by Richard Tames (Franklin Watts, 1989).
Mother Teresa: Friend of the Friendless, by Carol Greene (Children's Press, 1983).
Mother Teresa: A Sister to the Poor, by Patricia Reilly Giff (Viking Kestrel, 1986).

Books about India

Living in India, by Anne Singh (Young Discovery, 1988).
Take a Trip to India, by Keith Lye (Franklin Watts, 1982).
We Live in India, by Veenu Sandal (Franklin Watts, 1984).

Books for older readers

The Miracle of Love, by Kathryn Spink (Harper & Row, 1981).
Mother Teresa: A Simple Path, by Mother Teresa, compiled by Lucinda Vardey (Ballantine Books, 1995).
My Life for the Poor, by Mother Teresa of Calcutta (Harper & Row, 1985).
Such a Vision of the Street, by Eileen Egan (Doubleday, 1985).
Teresa of Calcutta, by Robert Serrou (McGraw-Hill, 1981).

Index